Design Directory

Eleganza Throw

Skill Level
 INTERMEDIATE

Finished Measurement
54 x 42 inches

Materials
Patons Divine bulky
   weight yarn (3½ oz/
   142 yds/100g per ball):
   5 balls Chantilly rose #06406
Size 15 (10mm) circular knitting
   needle or size needed to
   obtain gauge
Tapestry needle

Gauge
8 sts = 4 inches/10cm in pat
To save time, take time to
   check gauge.

Pattern Note
Circular needle is used to
   accommodate large number of
   sts, work back and forth in rows.
   Do not join.

Instructions

Cast on 82 sts.
Row 1 (RS row): Knit.
Row 2: K1, *p4, k8, p4; rep from * 4
   times, k1.
Row 3: K1, *yo, k3, ssk, p6, k2tog,
   k3, yo, rep from * 4 times, k1.
Row 4: K1, *p1-tbl, p4, k6, p5; rep
   from * 4 times, k1.
Row 5: K1, *k1, yo, k3, ssk, p4,
   k2tog, k3, yo, k1; rep from * 4
   times, k1.
Row 6: K1, *p6, k4, p6; rep from * 4
   times, k1.
Row 7: K1, *k2, yo, k3, ssk, p2,
   k2tog, k3, yo, k2; rep from * 4
   times, k1.
Row 8: K1, *p7, k2, p7; rep from * 4
   times, k1.
Row 9: K1, *k3, yo, k3, ssk, k2tog,
   k3, yo, k3; rep from * 4 times, k1.
Row 10: K1, purl to last st, k1.
Rep Rows 1 through 10 until throw
   measures about 50 inches,
   ending by working a Row 1.
Bind off as follows: K1, [p4, k8, p4] 5
   times, k1. ●

Embossed Diamonds

Skill Level
◼◼◼◻ INTERMEDIATE

Finished Measurement
40 x 55 inches

Materials
Red Heart Super Saver medium weight yarn (7 oz/364 yds/198g per skein): 7 skeins buff #334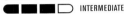
Size 17 (12.75mm) circular knitting needle or size needed to obtain gauge
Tapestry needle

Gauge
19 sts = 10 inches/25cm in garter st (knit every row) with 3 strands of yarn held tog
To save time, take time to check gauge.

Pattern Notes
Throw is worked with 3 strands of yarn held tog.
Circular needle is used to accommodate large number of sts, work back and forth in rows. Do not join.
Due to nature of pattern, finished throw will not be a perfect rectangle and will need to be blocked to given measurements. Knitted fabric tends to shrink horizontally.

Instructions

Cast on 91 sts.

Row 1 (RS): K3, *p2, k2, p1, k3, p1, k1, p1, k3, p1, k2, p2, k3; rep from * 3 times.

Row 2: K1, p1, *p1, k2, p2, k5, p1, k5, p2, k2, p2; rep from * 3 times, k1.

Rows 3 and 4: Rep Rows 1 and 2.

Row 5: K2, *p2, k2, (p1, k3) 3 times, p1, k2, p2, k1; rep from * 3 times, k1.

Row 6: K1, p1, *k2, p2, k5, p3, k5, p2, k2, p1; rep from * 3 times, k1.

Rows 7 and 8: Rep Rows 5 and 6.

Row 9: K1, p1, *p1, k2, p1, k3, [p1, k2] twice, p1, k3, p1, k2, p2; rep from * 3 times, k1.

Row 10: K3, *p2, k5, p2, k1, p2, k5, p2, k3; rep from * 3 times.

Rows 11 and 12: Rep Rows 9 and 10.

Row 13: K1, p1, *k2, p1, k3, p1, k2, p3, k2, p1, k3, p1, k2, p1; rep from * 3 times, k1.

Row 14: K2, *p2, k5, p2, k3, p2, k5, p2, k1; rep from * 3 times, k1.

Rows 15 and 16: Rep Rows 13 and 14.

Row 17: K3, *p1, k3, p1, k2, p2, k1, p2, k2, p1, k3, p1, k3; rep from 3 times.

Row 18: K1, p1, *p1, k5, p2, k2, p1, k2, p2, k5, p2; rep from * 3 times, k1.

Rows 19 and 20: Rep Rows 17 and 18.

Row 21: K2, *p1, k3, p1, k2, p2, k3, p2, k2, p1, k3, p1, k1; rep from * 3 times, k1.

Row 22: K1, p1, *k5, p2, k2, p3, k2, p2, k5, p1; rep from * 3 times, k1.

Rows 23 and 24: Rep Rows 21 and 22.

Row 25: K3, *p1, k3, p1, k2, p2, k1, p2, k2, p1, k3, p1, k3; rep from * 3 times.

Row 26: K1, p1, *p1, k5, p2, k2, p1, k2, p2, k5, p2; rep from * 3 times, k1.

Rows 27 and 28: Rep Rows 25 and 26.

Row 29: K1, p1, *k2, p1, k3, p1, k2, p3, k2, p1, k3, p1, k2, p1; rep from * 3 times, k1.

Row 30: K2, *p2, k5, p2, k3, p2, k5, p2, k1; rep from * 3 times, k1.

Rows 31 and 32: Rep Rows 29 and 30.

Row 33: K1, p1, *p1, k2, p1, k3, [p1, k2] twice, p1, k3, p1, k2, p2; rep from * 3 times, k1.

Row 34: K3, *p2, k5, p2, k1, p2, k5, p2, k3; rep from * 3 times.

Rows 35 and 36: Rep Rows 33 and 34.

Row 37: K2, *p2, k2, [p1, k3] 3 times, p1, k2, p2, k1; rep from * 3 times, k1.

Row 38: K1, p1, *k2, p2, k5, p3, k5, p2, k2, p1; rep from * 3 times, k1.

Rows 39 and 40: Rep Rows 37 and 38.

Rep Rows 1 through 40 until afghan measures about 55 inches, ending by working an even-numbered row.

Note: *When measuring, be sure afghan is flat and not stretched from weight of fabric.*

Bind off working next row of pattern.

Block throw to measure 40 x 55 inches. ●

Clear Skies

Skill Level
■ ■ ■ ▢ INTERMEDIATE

Finished Measurement
52 x 72 inches

Materials
Bernat Berella "4" medium weight yarn (3½ oz/ 195 yds/100g per ball): 22 balls true periwinkle blue #01142
Size 19 (15mm) circular knitting needle or size needed to obtain gauge
Tapestry needle

Gauge
7 sts = 4 inches/10cm in St st (k 1 row, p 1 row) with 3 strands of yarn held tog
To save time, take time to check gauge.

Pattern Notes
Afghan is worked with 3 strands of yarn held tog.
Circular needle is used to accommodate large number of sts, work back and forth in rows. Do not join.

Instructions

Cast on 93 sts.
Row 1 (RS): Knit.
Row 2: K5, *p11, k7; rep from * 3 times, p11, k5.
Row 3: K1, p4, *[k2tog] twice, [yo, k1] 3 times, yo, [ssk] twice, p7; rep from * 3 times, [k2tog] twice, [yo, k1] 3 times, yo, [ssk] twice, p4, k1.
Row 4: K1, p4, *k11, p7; rep from * 3 times, k11, p4, k1.
Row 5: Rep Row 2.
[Rep Rows 2–5] until afghan measures 72 inches, ending by working a Row 5.
Note: *When measuring, be sure afghan is flat and not stretched from weight of fabric.*
Bind off as follows: K5, *p11, k7; rep from * 3 times, p11, k5. ●

Tiger Stripes

Skill Level

◼◼◼◻ INTERMEDIATE

Finished Measurement

42 x 56 inches

Materials

Lion Brand Wool-Ease Chunky bulky weight yarn (5 oz/153 yds/140g per skein): 5 skeins each spice #135 (A) and pumpkin #133 (B), 1 skein black #153 (C)

Lion Brand Fancy Fur super bulky weight yarn (1¾ oz/39 yds/50g per ball): 3 balls jungle print #255 (D)

Size 35 (19mm) straight knitting needles, 14-inches long, or size needed to obtain gauge

Tapestry needle

Gauge

26 sts = 10 inches/25cm in pat st with 2 strands of yarn held tog

To save time, take time to check gauge.

Special Abbreviation

Inc (increase): Purl into front and back of next st.

Pattern Note

Afghan is worked with 2 strands of yarn held tog.

Instructions

With A, cast on 81 sts.

Row 1 (WS): K1, *[p2tog, (k1, p1, k1) in next st] 3 times, k1, [(k1, p1, k1) in next st, p2tog] 3 times, k1; rep from * 3 times. (105 sts)

Row 2: K1, *p2tog, p9, (inc) twice, p10, p2tog, p1; rep from * twice, p2tog, p9, (inc) twice, p10, p2tog, k1.

Row 3: K1, *[p3tog, (k1, p1, k1) in next st] 3 times, k1, [(k1, p1, k1) in next st, p3tog] 3 times, k1; rep from * 3 times.

Row 4: Rep row 2.

Rows 5–71: Rep Rows 3–4 in the following color sequence:

6 rows with 2 strands A.
2 rows with 1 strand each C and D.
10 rows with 2 strands B.
2 rows with 1 strand each C and D.
10 rows with 2 strands A.
2 rows with 1 strand each C and D.
10 rows with 2 strands B.
2 rows with 1 strand each C and D.
10 rows with 2 strands A.
2 rows with 1 strand each C and D.
11 rows with 2 strands B.

Bind off as follows: With B, k1 *[p2tog] twice, p1, p2tog, p10, p2tog, p2, [p2tog] twice, p1; rep from * twice, [p2tog] twice, p1, p2tog, p10, p2tog, p2, [p2tog] twice, k1. ●

Weekend Cabin

Skill Level
■■■□ INTERMEDIATE

Finished Measurement
46 x 60 inches

Materials
Red Heart Super Saver medium weight yarn (7 oz/364 yds/198g per skein): 4 skeins each Windsor blue #380 (A), gray heather #400 (B), light gray #341 (C)

Size 17 (12.75mm) circular knitting needle or size needed to obtain gauge

Tapestry needle

Gauge
18 sts = 10 inches/25cm in garter st (knit every row) with 3 strands of yarn held tog

To save time, take time to check gauge.

Pattern Notes
Afghan is worked with 3 strands of yarn held tog.

Circular needle is used to accommodate large number of sts, work back and forth in rows. Do not join.

Slip sts as if to purl wyib.

Number of sts will vary from row to row.

Instructions

With A, loosely cast on 81 sts.

Rows 1–3: Knit.

Row 4: K1, yo, sl 1, *k5, yo, sl 1; rep from * 12 times, k1. (95 sts)

Row 5: K2, sl 1 (yo from previous row), *k6, sl 1 (yo from previous row); rep from * 12 times, k1.

Row 6: K1, k2tog, *yo, sl 1, k3, yo, sl 1, k2tog; rep from * 12 times, k1. (107 sts)

Row 7: K2, *k1, sl 1 (yo from previous row), k4, sl 1 (yo from previous row), k1; rep from * 12 times, k1.

Row 8: K1, yo, sl 1, *k2tog, yo, sl 1, k1, yo, sl 1, k2tog, yo, sl 1; rep from * 12 times, k1. (121 sts)

Row 9: K2, sl 1 (yo from previous row), *[k2, sl 1 (yo from previous row)] 3 times; rep from * 12 times, k1.

Row 10: K1, k2tog, *[yo, sl 1, k2tog] 3 times; rep from * 12 times, k1. (120 sts)

Row 11: K1, *[k2, sl 1 (yo from previous row)] 3 times; rep from * 12 times, k2.

Row 12: K2, *[k2tog, yo, sl 1] twice, k2tog, k1; rep from * 12 times, k1. (107 sts)

Row 13: K2, *[k2, sl 1 (yo from previous row)] twice, k2; rep from * 12 times, k1.

Row 14: K2, *k1, k2tog, yo, sl 1, k2tog, k2; rep from * 12 times, k1. (94 sts)

Row 15: K2, *k3, sl 1 (yo from previous row), k3; rep from * 12 times, k1.

Row 16: K2, *k3, k2tog, k2; rep from * 12 times, k1. (81 sts)

Rows 17 and 18: Knit.

Rows 19–216: Rep Rows 1–18 in the following color sequence:
18 Rows B
18 Rows C
18 Rows A
18 Rows B
18 Rows C
18 Rows A
18 Rows B
18 Rows C
18 Rows A
18 Rows B
18 Rows C

Bind off loosely. ●

Sumptuous Slants

Skill Level
◼◼◼▢ INTERMEDIATE

Finished Measurement
52 x 75 inches

Materials
Red Heart Super Saver medium weight yarn (7 oz/364 yds/198g per skein): 9 skeins med. purple #528 (A)

Lion Brand Chenille Thick & Quick super bulky weight yarn (100 yds per skein): 1 skein each, purple #147 (B), eucalyptus #133 (C) and chocolate #125 (D)

Size 17 (12.75mm) circular knitting needle or size needed to obtain gauge

Size 15 (10mm) circular knitting needle

Tapestry needle

Gauge
19 sts = 10 inches/25cm in garter st (knit every row) with larger needle and 3 strands of medium weight yarn held tog

To save time, take time to check gauge.

Special Abbreviation
Inc (increase): Knit into front and back of next st.

Pattern Notes
Main pat is worked with 3 strands of A held tog, and stripes are worked with 1 strand of B, C or D.

Afghan is worked diagonally from lower left corner to upper right corner.

Circular needles are used to accommodate large number of sts, work back and forth in rows. Do not join.

Due to nature of pattern, finished afghan will not be a perfect rectangle and will need to be blocked to given measurements.

Instructions

With larger needle and A, cast on 3 sts.

Row 1 (RS): K1, yo, k2. (4 sts)

Row 2: K1, yo, k2tog, yo, k1. (5 sts)

Row 3: K2, yo, k2tog, yo, k1. (6 sts)

Row 4: K2, yo, k2tog, yo, k2. (7 sts)

Row 5: K1, *yo, k2tog; rep from * to last 2 sts, yo, k2. (8 sts)

Row 6: K1, *yo, k2tog; rep from * to last st, yo, k1. (9 sts)

Row 7: K2, *yo, k2tog; rep from * to last st, yo, k1. (10 sts)

Row 8: K2, *yo, k2tog; rep from * to last 2 sts, yo, k2. (11 sts)

Rows 9–28: [Rep Rows 5–8] 5 times. (31 sts)

Cut A, join B.

Change to smaller needle.

Rows 29 and 30: Knit to last st, inc. (33 sts)

Cut B, join C.

Rows 31–34: Rep Row 29. (37 sts)

Cut C, join B.

Rows 35 and 36: Rep Row 29. (39 sts)

Cut B, join A.

Row 37: Rep Row 29. (40 sts)

Change to larger needle.

Rows 38–40: Rep Rows 6–8. (43 sts)

Rows 41–68: [Rep Rows 5–8] 7 times. (71 sts)

Cut A, join B.

Change to smaller needle.

Rows 69 and 70: Rep Row 29. (73 sts)

Cut B, join D.

Rows 71–74: Rep Row 29. (77 sts)

Cut D, join B.

Rows 75 and 76: Rep Row 29. (79 sts)

Cut B, join A.

Row 77: Rep Row 29. (80 sts)

Change to larger needle.

Rows 78–80: Rep Rows 6–8. (83 sts)

Rows 81–108: [Rep Rows 5–8] 7 times. (111 sts)

Cut A, join B.

Change to smaller needle.

Rows 109 and 110: Rep Row 29. (113 sts)

Cut B, join C.

Rows 111–114: Rep Row 29. (117 sts)

Cut C, join B.

Row 115: Rep Row 29. (118 sts)

Row 116: Knit to last 2 sts, k2tog. (117 sts)

Cut B, join A.

Row 117: Rep Row 29. (118 sts)

Change to larger needle.

Row 118: K1, *yo, k2tog; rep from * to last st, k1.

Row 119: K1, *k2tog, yo; rep from * to last st, k1.

Row 120: K2, *yo, k2tog; rep from * to last 2 sts, k2.

Row 121: K2, *k2tog, yo; rep from * to last 2 sts, k2.

Rows 122–145: [Rep Rows 118–121] 6 times.

Rows 146–148: Rep Rows 118–120.

Cut A, join B.

Change to smaller needle.

Row 149: Knit.

Row 150: Rep Row 116. (117 sts)

Cut B, join D.
Rows 151–154: Rep Row 116. (113 sts)
Cut D, join B.
Rows 155 and 156: Rep Row 116. (111 sts)
Cut B, join A.
Row 157: Rep Row 116. (110 sts)
Change to larger needle.
Row 158: K2, *k2tog, yo; rep from * to last 4 sts, k2tog, k2. (109 sts)
Row 159: K2, *k2tog, yo; rep from * to last 3 sts, k2tog, k1. (108 sts)
Row 160: K1, *k2tog, yo; rep from * to last 3 sts, k2tog, k1. (107 sts)
Row 161: K1, *k2tog, yo; rep from * to last 4 sts, k2tog, k2. (106 sts)
Rows 162–185: [Rep Row 158–161] 6 times. (82 sts)
Rows 186–188: Rep Rows 158–160. (79 sts)

Cut A, join B.
Change to smaller needle.
Rows 189 and 190: Rep Row 116. (77 sts)
Cut B, join C.
Rows 191–194: Rep Row 116. (73 sts)
Cut C, join B.
Rows 195 and 196: Rep Row 116. (71 sts)
Cut B, join A.
Row 197: Rep Row 116. (70 sts)
Change to larger needle.
Rows 198–225: [Rep Rows 158–161] 7 times. (42 sts)
Rows 226–228: Rep Rows 158–160. (39 sts)
Cut A, join B.
Change to smaller needle.
Rows 229 and 230: Rep Row 116. (37 sts)

Cut B, join D.
Rows 231–234: Rep Row 116. (33 sts)
Cut D, join B.
Rows 235 and 236: Rep Row 116. (31 sts)
Cut B, join A.
Row 237: Rep Row 116. (30 sts)
Change to larger needle.
Rows 238–261: [Rep Rows 158–161] 6 times. (6 sts)
Row 262: K2, k2tog, k2. (5 sts)
Row 263: K2, k2tog, k1. (4 sts)
Row 264: K1, k2tog, k1. (3 sts)
Row 265: K3tog.
Cut yarn and pull through.
Block afghan to measure 52 x 75 inches. ●

General Information

Knit Abbreviations & Symbols

approx · · · · · · approximately
beg · · · · · · begin/beginning
CC · · · · · · · contrasting color
ch · · · · · · · · chain stitch
cm · · · · · · · centimeter(s)
cn · · · · · · · · cable needle
dec · · · · decrease/decreases/ decreasing
dpn(s) · ·double-pointed needle(s)
g · · · · · · · · · · · gram
inc · increase/increases/increasing
k · · · · · · · · · · · · · knit
k2tog · · knit 2 stitches together
LH · · · · · · · · · · · ·left hand
lp(s) · · · · · · · · · · loop(s)
m · · · · · · · · · · ·meter(s)
M1 · · · · · · · · make one stitch
MC · · · · · · · · · · main color
mm · · · · · · · · · millimeter(s)
oz · · · · · · · · · · ounce(s)
p · · · · · · · · · · · ·purl

pat(s) · · · · · · · · · ·pattern(s)
p2tog · · · purl 2 stitches together
psso · · · · pass slipped stitch over
p2sso · · pass 2 slipped stitches over
rem · · · · · · · remain/remaining
rep · · · · · · · · · · repeat(s)
rev St st · · reverse stockinette stitch
RH · · · · · · · · · · right hand
rnd(s) · · · · · · · · · rounds
RS · · · · · · · · · · right side
skp · · ·slip, knit, pass stitch over— one stitch decreased
sk2p · · · · ·slip 1, knit 2 together, pass slip stitch over, then knit 2 together—2 stitches have been decreased
sl · · · · · · · · · · · · ·slip
sl 1k · · · · · · · · slip 1 knitwise
sl 1p · · · · · · · slip 1 purlwise
sl st · · · · · · · slip stitch(es)
ssk · · slip, slip, knit these 2 stitches together—a decrease

st(s) · · · · · · · · · stitch(es)
St st · · · · · stockinette stitch/ stocking stitch
tbl · · · · · through back loop(s)
tog · · · · · · · · · ·together
WS · · · · · · · · · wrong side
wyib · · · · · with yarn in back
wyif · · · · · with yarn in front
yd(s) · · · · · · · · · yard(s)
yfwd · · · · · · · yarn forward
yo(s) · · · · · · · yarn over(s)

[] work instructions within brackets as many times as directed
() work instructions within parentheses in the place directed
** repeat instructions following the asterisks as directed
* repeat instructions following the single asterisk as directed
" inch(es)

Standard Yarn Weight System

Categories of yarn, gauge ranges, and recommended needle sizes

Yarn Weight Symbol & Category Names	1 SUPER FINE	2 FINE	3 LIGHT	4 MEDIUM	5 BULKY	6 SUPER BULKY
Type of Yarns in Category	Sock, Fingering, Baby	Sport, Baby	DK, Light Worsted	Worsted, Afghan, Aran	Chunky, Craft, Rug	Bulky, Roving
Knit Gauge Range* in Stockinette Stitch to 4 inches	27–32 sts	23–26 sts	21–24 sts	16–20 sts	12–15 sts	6–11 sts
Recommended Needle in Metric Size Range	2.25–3.25mm	3.25–3.75mm	3.75–4.5mm	4.5–5.5mm	5.5–8mm	8mm and larger
Recommended Needle U.S. Size Range	1 to 3	3 to 5	5 to 7	7 to 9	9 to 11	11 and larger

* GUIDELINES ONLY: The above reflect the most commonly used gauges and needle sizes for specific yarn categories.

How to Check Gauge

A correct stitch gauge is very important. Please take the time to work a stitch gauge swatch about 4 x 4 inches. Measure the swatch. If the number of stitches and rows are fewer than indicated under "Gauge" in the pattern, your needles are too large. Try another swatch with smaller-size needles. If the number of stitches and rows are more than indicated under "Gauge" in the pattern, your needles are too small. Try another swatch with larger-size needles.

Skill Levels

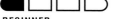

BEGINNER
Beginner projects for first-time knitters using basic stitches. Minimal shaping.

EASY
Easy projects using basic stitches, repetitive stitch patterns, simple color changes and simple shaping and finishing.

INTERMEDIATE
Intermediate projects with a variety of stitches, mid-level shaping and finishing.

EXPERIENCED
Experienced projects using advanced techniques and stitches, detailed shaping and refined finishing.

Inches Into Millimeters & Centimeters
All measurements are rounded off slightly.

inches	mm	cm	inches	cm	inches	cm	inches	cm
⅛	3	0.3	5	12.5	21	53.5	38	96.5
¼	6	0.6	5½	14	22	56.0	39	99.0
⅜	10	1.0	6	15.0	23	58.5	40	101.5
½	13	1.3	7	18.0	24	61.0	41	104.0
⅝	15	1.5	8	20.5	25	63.5	42	106.5
¾	20	2.0	9	23.0	26	66.0	43	109.0
⅞	22	2.2	10	25.5	27	68.5	44	112.0
1	25	2.5	11	28.0	28	71.0	45	114.5
1¼	32	3.8	12	30.5	29	73.5	46	117.0
1½	38	3.8	13	33.0	30	76.0	47	119.5
1¾	45	4.5	14	35.5	31	79.0	48	122.0
2	50	5.0	15	38.0	32	81.5	49	124.5
2½	65	6.5	16	40.5	33	84.0	50	127.0
3	75	7.5	17	43.0	34	86.5		
3½	90	9.0	18	46.0	35	89.0		
4	100	10.0	19	48.5	36	91.5		
4½	115	11.5	20	51.0	37	94.0		

Knitting Needle Conversion Chart

U.S.	1	2	3	4	5	6	7	8	9	10	10½	11	13	15	17	19	35	50
Continental-mm	2.25	2.75	3.25	3.5	3.75	4	4.5	5	5.5	6	6.5	8	9	10	12.75	15	19	25

American
School of
Needlework ®
excellence
in instruction

TOLL-FREE ORDER LINE or to request a free catalog (800) 582-6643
Customer Service (800) 282-6643, **Fax** (800) 882-6643
Visit DRGnetwork.com.

We have made every effort to ensure the accuracy and completeness of these instructions.
We cannot, however, be responsible for human error, typographical mistakes or variations in individual work.

ISBN: 978-1-59012-207-5   All rights reserved.   Printed in USA   1 2 3 4 5 6 7 8 9